HAYLEY HAYES

Digital Identity Unlocked

Mastering Personal Branding in the Online World

This book was professionally typeset on Reedsy.
Find out more at reedsy.com

Contents

1

Introduction

In the exhilarating landscape of the digital world, where endless opportunities await at your fingertips, "Digital Identity Unlocked: Mastering Personal Branding in the Online World" is your indispensable guide. Picture this: a reality where you, whether a budding entrepreneur, a driven professional, or a digital enthusiast, wield the power of the online realm to carve out a personal brand that's not only authentic but also immensely impactful and rewarding.

In these pages, you'll find more than just a book; it's a compact, easy-to-use toolkit designed to fit right into your busy life. We're here to provide you with a straightforward map to navigate the ever-changing digital terrain. From understanding the nuts and bolts of your digital identity to mastering the art of personal branding and optimizing your online presence, this book covers it all. But that's not all – we'll also explore how to skillfully navigate the challenges and pitfalls that come with the territory.

Think of this book as your personal mentor, guiding you through real-life case studies and success stories that will not only educate but also inspire you. Our aim? To equip you with the knowledge, strategies, and insights necessary to confidently build a personal brand that resonates with your core values, aligns with your goals, and connects with your desired audience.

So, whether you're a tech-savvy marketer, a creative designer, an ambitious freelancer, or a job seeker looking to make your mark, this book is tailored for you. It's crafted for the college-educated, the career-driven, the digital trendsetters – essentially, anyone who's eager to embrace professional growth and personal authenticity in the online world.

As we embark on this journey together, remember: the digital landscape is more than a space; it's a canvas, and you're the artist. Let's unlock the full potential of your digital identity and paint a masterpiece that is uniquely you.

2

Understanding Your Digital Identity

We dive deep into the concept of digital identity, a critical aspect of personal and professional branding in the online world. We start by defining what digital identity entails, then explore its evolution alongside the rise of online platforms, and finally, assess the significant impact of social media on how we form and perceive our identities.

Defining Digital Identity

In the digital era, understanding your digital identity is crucial. It's not just an online version of who you are; it's a multifaceted representation of your personality, beliefs, and achievements that exists in the digital world. Here's how to understand and define your digital identity:

What is Digital Identity?

- **A Composite Picture:** Your digital identity is a composite of various elements such as your social media profiles, blog posts, comments, online transactions, and even the emails you send. It's how you present yourself and are perceived in the digital realm.
- **Dynamic and Evolving:** Unlike a static ID card, your digital identity is dynamic, evolving with every post, like, share, and comment. It reflects your current interests, opinions, and interactions.

Components of Your Digital Identity:

- **Profiles and Personal Information:** This includes basic information like your name, photo, and bio across various platforms, but also your professional history on sites like LinkedIn.
- **Content and Contributions:** The articles you write, the tweets you share, the comments you make on forums – all these contribute to painting a picture of your interests, expertise, and personality.
- **Interactions and Connections:** Your digital identity is also shaped by who you interact with online, the networks you're part of, and how you engage with others' content.

Reflecting Your True Self:

- **Authenticity vs. Curation:** It's important to balance authenticity with curation. While it's natural to want to present your best self online, ensuring that your digital identity aligns with your real-life values and personality is key.

- **Consistency Across Platforms:** Consistency in how you present yourself across different platforms strengthens your digital identity. This doesn't mean being monotonous, but ensuring a coherent narrative.

Understanding the Impact of Your Digital Footprint:

- **Long-term Implications:** Every digital interaction leaves a trace. Being mindful of this digital footprint is crucial, as it can have long-term implications on your personal and professional life.
- **Privacy Considerations:** Regularly review privacy settings on social platforms and be conscious of the information you share publicly. Your digital identity should be a conscious expression of who you are and how you wish to be perceived.

Evolving with Technology:

- **Staying Up-to-date:** As technology evolves, so do the platforms and means of expressing your digital identity. Stay informed about new platforms and trends to understand how they might affect or enhance your digital presence.

The Evolution of Personal Branding Online

Understanding the evolution of personal branding online is crucial for anyone looking to establish a strong presence in the digital world. This journey from simple online profiles to complex, multifaceted digital personas highlights the changing landscape of personal branding. Here's a breakdown of this evolution to help you navigate and adapt your own branding strategy:

The Early Days of the Internet:

- **From Anonymity to Recognition:** In the early days of the internet, online interactions were largely anonymous. Personal branding was confined to basic user profiles on forums or chat rooms, with limited scope for individual expression.
- **Rise of Personal Websites:** The advent of personal websites and blogs marked a shift, allowing individuals to showcase their skills, interests, and expertise more broadly, laying the groundwork for personal branding.

Social Media: A Game Changer:

- **Platforms for Self-Expression:** The emergence of social media platforms like MySpace, Facebook, and LinkedIn revolutionized personal branding. These platforms gave individuals a stage to craft and project a more defined personal image and narrative.
- **Diverse Audiences and Interactions:** As these platforms evolved, they catered to different audiences and interac-

tions, from professional networking on LinkedIn to more personal, casual interactions on Facebook and Twitter.

Content Creation and Branding:

- **Blogging and Video Content:** The rise of blogging and platforms like YouTube allowed for more dynamic content creation, enabling individuals to build personal brands around their expertise, hobbies, or lifestyle.
- **Authenticity and Engagement:** This era emphasized the importance of authenticity, with successful personal brands often built on genuine engagement and unique, relatable content.

Integration of Multimedia:

- **Visual and Interactive Content:** The integration of multimedia (images, videos, interactive posts) on platforms like Instagram and TikTok further expanded the scope of personal branding. These tools allowed for more visually driven and engaging content, crucial for brand differentiation.
- **Personal Storytelling:** The use of multimedia enabled more effective storytelling, allowing individuals to craft more immersive and emotionally engaging narratives.

The Current Landscape:

- **Data-Driven Personal Branding:** The current landscape of personal branding is heavily influenced by data analytics. Understanding metrics and audience insights on various

platforms can guide content strategy and engagement.
- **Omnichannel Presence:** Establishing a presence across multiple platforms (omnichannel branding) is now standard. Coherent and consistent messaging across these platforms strengthens brand identity.

Looking Ahead:

- **Technological Advancements:** The future of personal branding is likely to be shaped further by technological advancements like AI, augmented reality, and virtual reality, offering new avenues for brand expression and engagement.
- **Adaptability and Continuous Learning:** Staying adaptable and continually learning about new platforms and technologies will be key to maintaining a relevant and impactful personal brand.

The Impact of Social Media on Identity Formation

In today's digital age, social media plays a pivotal role in shaping our identities. Understanding the impact of these platforms on identity formation is crucial for anyone looking to harness their power for personal branding. This section explores how social media influences our digital identities and how you can use it to your advantage.

Crafting a Digital Self:

- **Social Media as a Canvas:** Social media provides a canvas for expressing different facets of your identity. Each platform offers unique tools and audiences, allowing you to craft and project various aspects of your personality, interests, and professional life.
- **The Balance of Personal and Professional:** It's important to strike a balance between personal expression and professional branding. Understanding the tone and audience of each platform helps in tailoring your content to suit both personal and professional aspects of your identity.

The Power of Storytelling:

- **Narrative Construction:** Social media enables you to construct a narrative about who you are. Through posts, stories, images, and videos, you can tell your story in a way that resonates with your audience, building a connection that goes beyond just professional interactions.
- **Authenticity and Engagement:** The most impactful social media identities are built on authenticity. Being genuine in your storytelling fosters engagement and builds trust with your audience.

The Influence of Community and Networks:

- **Building a Community:** Social media allows you to build communities around shared interests, professions, or beliefs. This not only helps in identity formation but also in establishing a support network.

- **Learning from Interaction:** The interactions you have on social media, both positive and negative, can shape your digital identity. Engaging with feedback and adapting your approach based on these interactions are key in evolving your online persona.

Managing Online Reputation:

- **Consistency Across Platforms:** Consistency in your online behavior across different platforms is essential in maintaining a coherent digital identity. This involves aligning your messaging, values, and even visual style across various social media.
- **Dealing with Negativity:** Handling negative comments or feedback professionally and gracefully is an important aspect of managing your online reputation and, by extension, your digital identity.

Adapting to Social Media Evolution:

- **Staying Updated with Trends:** Social media is constantly evolving, with new platforms, features, and trends emerging regularly. Staying informed and adaptable to these changes is crucial for keeping your digital identity relevant.
- **Continuous Learning and Experimentation:** Experimenting with new platforms and features, while continuously learning about best practices in social media, can help in enhancing and refining your digital identity.

3

Building Your Personal Brand

This chapter is dedicated to guiding you through the process of building your personal brand. We'll cover everything from identifying your unique brand proposition to crafting your online narrative, choosing the right platforms, creating engaging content, and interacting with your audience.

Identifying Your Unique Brand Proposition

In the realm of personal branding, your unique brand proposition (UBP) is what sets you apart from others in your field. It's the distinct combination of skills, experiences, and personality traits that make you unique. This section is dedicated to helping you identify and articulate your UBP, a crucial step in establishing a memorable and impactful personal brand.

Understanding the Concept of a Unique Brand Proposition:

- **Definition of UBP:** Start by understanding what a UBP is — it's essentially your personal brand's unique selling point. It's what you offer that no one else can, your individual mark in your professional field.
- **The Importance of UBP:** Your UBP is what will make you stand out in a crowded digital space. It's the key to differentiating yourself from the competition and creating a lasting impression on your audience.

Self-Reflection and Discovery:

- **Identifying Your Strengths and Passions:** Reflect on your strengths, skills, and areas of expertise. What are you exceptionally good at? Also, consider your passions. Often, the intersection of your skills and passions is where your UBP lies.
- **Evaluating Your Experiences:** Consider your unique life and professional experiences. How have these shaped you? What unique perspectives have they given you? Your unique experiences often contribute significantly to your UBP.

Aligning UBP with Professional Goals:

- **Career Aspirations and UBP:** It's essential that your UBP aligns with your career aspirations. If your goal is to be a thought leader in digital marketing, for example, your UBP should reflect your expertise and innovative thinking in that area.

- **Target Audience Relevance:** Your UBP should resonate with your target audience. Understand who you are trying to reach and what they value. This alignment ensures that your UBP not only distinguishes you but also appeals to those you wish to influence or serve.

Articulating Your UBP:

- **Crafting a Clear UBP Statement:** Once you've identified your UBP, the next step is to articulate it clearly and concisely. This statement should encapsulate what makes you unique and valuable in your field.
- **Incorporating Your UBP into Your Brand:** Your UBP should be evident in every aspect of your personal brand, from your social media profiles to the content you create. Consistently communicate your UBP across all platforms.

Seeking Feedback and Refinement:

- **Gathering External Perspectives:** Sometimes, external feedback can provide insights into aspects of your brand that you may not have considered. Seek feedback from colleagues, mentors, or peers to refine your UBP.
- **Continual Refinement:** Your UBP is not static. As you grow professionally and personally, revisit and refine your UBP to ensure it remains relevant and reflective of who you are.

Crafting Your Online Narrative

Crafting your online narrative is about telling your story in a way that's both consistent and authentic, reflecting who you are and what you stand for. It's a crucial component of your personal brand, allowing you to connect with your audience on a deeper level. Here's how to effectively craft and convey your narrative online:

Understanding the Importance of an Online Narrative:

- **Narrative as a Branding Tool:** Your online narrative is more than just a collection of random posts and updates. It's a strategic tool that communicates your journey, values, and expertise to your audience.
- **Impact on Audience Perception:** A well-crafted narrative shapes how others perceive you. It can influence your credibility, relatability, and the opportunities that come your way.

Elements of a Compelling Narrative:

- **Personal Journey and Milestones:** Share your journey, including the milestones and challenges you've faced. This not only showcases your achievements but also humanizes you, making your story relatable.
- **Values and Passions:** Infuse your narrative with your core values and passions. This gives your audience insights into what drives you and what matters to you, building a deeper connection.

Consistency Across Platforms:

- **Unified Message:** Ensure your narrative is consistent across different platforms. Whether it's LinkedIn, Twitter, or Instagram, each post should contribute to a cohesive story about who you are.
- **Visual Consistency:** Maintain visual consistency in your profile pictures, cover images, and the overall aesthetic of your content. This helps in creating a recognizable and memorable brand.

Authenticity in Storytelling:

- **Genuine Content:** Be authentic in what you share. Authenticity resonates with audiences more than perfection. Share your successes, but also be open about struggles and failures.
- **Voice and Tone:** Use a voice and tone that are true to you. Whether it's professional, conversational, or a mix of both, it should reflect your real-life personality.

Engaging with Your Audience:

- **Interactive Storytelling:** Make your narrative interactive by engaging with your audience. Respond to comments, ask for feedback, and participate in conversations. This interaction brings your story to life.
- **Incorporating Audience Feedback:** Use feedback from your audience to evolve your narrative. Understanding what resonates with them can help you refine your story and make it more impactful.

Regular Updates and Adaptation:

- **Evolving Your Narrative:** As you grow and evolve, so should your narrative. Regularly update your story to reflect new experiences, skills, and perspectives.
- **Staying Relevant:** Stay abreast of current trends and adapt your narrative to remain relevant. This doesn't mean changing your core story, but rather finding ways to connect it with current conversations and trends.

Utilizing Different Platforms (LinkedIn, Twitter, Instagram, Facebook, YouTube, etc.)

Effectively utilizing various social media platforms is key to creating a cohesive brand image. Each platform offers unique opportunities to showcase different aspects of your personal brand. Here's how to approach each major platform with specific strategies:

LinkedIn: The Professional Hub

- **Optimize Your Profile:** Ensure your LinkedIn profile is complete with a professional photo, detailed work experience, and a compelling summary. Utilize keywords relevant to your industry for better visibility.
- **Content Strategy:** Share professional insights, write articles, and engage with content in your field. LinkedIn is ideal for demonstrating your professional expertise and thought leadership.

Twitter: The Pulse of Conversation

- **Consistent Voice:** Develop a consistent voice and tone suitable for the fast-paced nature of Twitter. Be it professional, witty, or a mix, ensure it aligns with your overall brand personality.
- **Engagement and Networking:** Use Twitter to engage in industry conversations, network with peers, and share timely content. Regularly participating in relevant hashtag conversations can increase your visibility.

Instagram: The Visual Storyteller

- **Aesthetic Consistency:** Maintain a consistent visual aesthetic on your Instagram feed. Use a specific color scheme or filter to create a recognizable look.
- **Storytelling Through Images:** Leverage Instagram to tell your story visually. Share behind-the-scenes content, personal achievements, and moments that reflect your brand's personality.

Facebook: Building Communities

- **Personal Meets Professional:** Facebook allows for a blend of personal and professional content. Share updates that showcase your personality but also align with your professional brand.
- **Groups and Pages:** Engage with or create Facebook Groups relevant to your industry. These can be great for establishing authority and connecting with a like-minded community.

YouTube: Engaging Through Video

- **Content Quality:** Focus on the quality of your video content. Videos should reflect your professional image and be relevant to your audience's interests.
- **Consistent Posting Schedule:** Maintain a regular posting schedule. Consistent uploads can help in building a loyal audience and enhance your brand presence.

Creating a Cohesive Brand Image Across Platforms:

- **Unified Messaging:** While your content can vary across platforms, the underlying message should be unified. Ensure that your core values and brand proposition are consistently reflected.
- **Cross-Platform Promotion:** Promote your content across different platforms. For instance, share your latest YouTube video on LinkedIn or tweet about your recent Instagram post. This helps in creating an interconnected brand presence.

Adapting to Each Platform's Unique Environment:

- **Understand Each Platform's Culture:** Each social media platform has its unique culture and norms. Tailor your content to fit the environment of each platform while maintaining your brand's voice and message.
- **Experiment and Adapt:** Don't be afraid to experiment with different types of content to see what resonates best with each platform's audience. Adapt based on engagement and feedback.

Content Creation Strategies

Developing a content plan that emphasizes quality and originality is essential for reinforcing your personal brand and engaging your audience effectively. Here's how to create a content strategy that resonates with your audience while staying true to your brand.

Defining Your Content Goals:

- **Establish Clear Objectives:** Start by defining what you want to achieve with your content. Are you looking to establish thought leadership, share industry insights, or showcase your creative work? Setting clear goals will guide your content creation process.
- **Aligning with Your Brand:** Ensure your content goals align with your overall personal brand. Every piece of content should reinforce the message and values you want to convey.

Understanding Your Audience:

- **Identify Your Target Audience:** Know who your content is for. Understanding your audience's interests, needs, and challenges will help you create content that resonates with them.
- **Engaging with Audience Feedback:** Pay attention to comments, shares, and feedback. Audience engagement is a valuable source of insight and can inform your future content.

Content Quality Over Quantity:

- **Focus on High-Quality Content:** Prioritize creating content that is well-researched, well-produced, and provides value. Quality content will position you as a reliable source in your field.
- **Consistency in Posting:** While quality is crucial, consistency is also key. Develop a content calendar to maintain a steady flow of content without compromising quality.

Originality and Creativity:

- **Showcase Your Unique Perspective:** Bring your unique insights or angle to your content. Originality sets you apart and makes your content memorable.
- **Experiment with Different Formats:** Don't be afraid to experiment with various content formats like blogs, videos, podcasts, or infographics. Different formats can bring out different aspects of your brand.

Leveraging SEO and Keywords:

- **Optimize for Search Engines:** Use relevant keywords and SEO best practices to increase the visibility of your content online. This is especially important for written content like blogs and articles.
- **Stay Updated on SEO Trends:** SEO is continually evolving. Keep yourself updated on the latest trends and algorithm changes to ensure your content remains discoverable.

Promotion and Distribution:

- **Utilize Multiple Channels:** Don't limit your content to one platform. Distribute and promote your content across various channels where your audience is present.
- **Cross-Promotion:** Leverage your presence on one platform to promote content on another. For instance, share snippets of a blog post on LinkedIn or Twitter to drive traffic to your website.

Measuring Success and Adapting:

- **Track Engagement and Metrics:** Use analytics tools to track the performance of your content. Metrics like views, shares, and engagement rates can provide insights into what works.
- **Adapt Based on Feedback:** Be prepared to adapt your content strategy based on what the analytics tell you. Continuous learning and adaptation are key to a successful content strategy.

Engaging with Your Audience

Engaging with your audience is not just about sharing content; it's about building relationships and creating a community around your personal brand. Effective audience engagement can lead to increased brand loyalty, valuable feedback, and a deeper understanding of your audience. Here are specific strategies to help you engage effectively with your audience:

Active Listening and Responsiveness:

- **Monitor and Respond to Comments:** Regularly monitor comments on your posts and respond in a timely manner. This shows your audience that you value their input and are approachable.
- **Acknowledge Feedback:** Whether positive or negative, acknowledging feedback demonstrates that you are receptive and committed to your audience's experience.

Creating Interactive Content:

- **Ask Questions and Encourage Participation:** Create posts that invite your audience to engage, such as asking for their opinions, thoughts, or experiences related to your content.
- **Polls and Surveys:** Utilize polls and surveys to gather opinions and insights. This not only engages your audience but can also provide valuable data for future content.

Leveraging Social Media Features:

- **Use Stories and Live Sessions:** Platforms like Instagram and Facebook offer 'Stories' and live streaming features that are excellent for real-time engagement. Host Q&A sessions, share behind-the-scenes content, or simply have a live chat with your audience.
- **Join or Create Groups:** Participate in or create Facebook or LinkedIn groups related to your industry. These can be great platforms for deeper discussions and community building.

Personalization and Direct Interaction:

- **Direct Messages:** Use direct messages to interact with your audience on a more personal level. Personalized responses can significantly boost audience loyalty.
- **Tailor Content to Audience Interests:** Use insights gained from audience interactions to tailor your content to their interests, making your posts more relevant and engaging.

Consistent Community Engagement:

- **Regular Engagement:** Consistently engage with your community by commenting on their posts, sharing their content, and acknowledging their milestones. This helps in building a strong and supportive community.
- **Community Events:** Host or participate in community events, webinars, or online discussions. This can help in strengthening connections and increasing engagement.

User-Generated Content and Collaborations:

- **Encourage User-Generated Content:** Prompt your audience to share their own content related to your brand, such as testimonials or how they use your advice in their daily life.
- **Collaborate with Other Influencers:** Collaborate with influencers or peers in your field to tap into their audience and bring fresh perspectives to your content.

Analyzing Engagement Patterns:

- **Use Analytics Tools:** Utilize analytics tools to understand which types of posts are generating the most engagement. This can help you refine your strategy and focus on what works best.
- **Adapt Based on Insights:** Be flexible and willing to adapt your engagement strategies based on what the data shows. Audience preferences can change, and staying adaptable is key.

4

Optimizing Your Digital Presence

We will focus on optimizing your digital presence. This step is crucial in ensuring that your personal brand is not only visible but also impactful and aligned with your goals.

SEO and Your Personal Brand

Understanding and leveraging Search Engine Optimization (SEO) is crucial for enhancing the visibility and impact of your personal brand online. This section delves into how you can use SEO strategies to ensure that your personal brand stands out in the digital landscape.

Understanding SEO Basics:

- **What is SEO?**: Begin by understanding what SEO is – it's the practice of increasing the quantity and quality of traffic to your website through organic search engine results.

- **Relevance to Personal Branding:** For personal branding, SEO helps ensure that when someone searches for your name or the skills and services you offer, they find relevant and accurate information. This can greatly enhance your professional credibility and visibility.

Keywords and Personal Branding:

- **Identifying Your Keywords:** Identify keywords that are relevant to your personal brand. These might include your industry, job title, key skills, and location. Think about what terms a potential employer, client, or collaborator might use to find someone with your expertise.
- **Incorporating Keywords:** Once you've identified your keywords, incorporate them into your digital content. This includes your LinkedIn profile, personal website, blog posts, and even your social media bios. However, it's crucial to use them naturally – stuffing your content with keywords can be counterproductive.

Optimizing Your Online Profiles:

- **Profile Optimization for Visibility:** Ensure that your online profiles are fully optimized. This means completing all available fields with detailed, accurate, and keyword-rich information about yourself. On platforms like LinkedIn, this includes your headline, summary, and experience sections.
- **Consistent NAP (Name, Address, Phone Number):** Consistency in your basic details across the web helps search engines recognize and correctly list your content.

Ensure your name and contact information are uniform across platforms.

Creating SEO-Friendly Content:

- **Blogging and Article Writing:** Regularly publishing blogs or articles on platforms like LinkedIn or your personal website can boost your SEO. These pieces should be informative, relevant to your field, and include your identified keywords.
- **Using Keywords Strategically:** While it's important to include keywords, they should be integrated seamlessly into your content. Overuse of keywords can make your content seem artificial and may negatively impact readability.

Building Online Visibility:

- **Engaging with Other Websites:** Engaging with other websites, such as guest blogging or participating in forums, can increase your visibility. Linking back to your website or profile where appropriate can drive traffic and improve your search rankings.
- **Social Media Activity:** Active participation in social media can also contribute to your SEO efforts. Regular posts, interactions, and sharing of your professional content can increase your online footprint.

Balancing Professionalism and Personality

Creating a balance between professionalism and personality in your online presence is key to building a relatable yet credible personal brand. This section explores how you can showcase your professional expertise while also letting your authentic personality shine through, enhancing both authenticity and engagement.

Professional Image vs. Personal Touch:

- **Understanding the Balance:** Professionalism in your online presence relates to how you showcase your expertise, achievements, and competence. Personality, on the other hand, involves infusing your unique character, interests, and viewpoints into your content. Finding the right balance ensures that you are seen as both skilled and approachable.
- **Crafting Your Online Persona:** Consider your online persona as a blend of your professional qualifications and your personal attributes. This persona should reflect the professionalism expected in your field, while also offering a glimpse into your personal life or interests in a manner that is appropriate and relatable.

Authenticity in Professionalism:

- **Being Genuine:** Authenticity is about being genuine in what you present online. Share real stories and experiences that highlight both your professional journey and personal growth. This could include challenges you've overcome, lessons learned, and milestones achieved.

- **Consistency in Your Storytelling:** Ensure that your stories and content remain consistent with your real-life experiences and values. Authenticity is key in building trust and credibility with your audience.

Engagement Through Personality:

- **Personalized Interaction:** Engage with your audience in a personalized manner. Respond to comments and messages in a way that reflects your personality, whether it's thoughtful, witty, or empathetic.
- **Sharing Personal Interests:** Don't hesitate to share your hobbies, interests, or causes you are passionate about. This helps in humanizing your brand and makes you more relatable to your audience.

Professional Boundaries:

- **Setting Limits:** While it's important to show personality, it's also crucial to set boundaries. Be mindful of the information you share and ensure it aligns with how you wish to be perceived professionally.
- **Tactful Sharing:** Share personal aspects of your life tactfully. This means considering the implications of what you share and how it might be perceived in a professional context.

29

Incorporating Visuals and Media:

- **Visual Consistency:** Use visuals that reflect both your professional expertise and personal style. This could include a professional headshot with a touch of personal flair or graphics and designs that match your personal brand.
- **Multimedia Content:** Consider using various forms of media, like videos or podcasts, to express your personality. This can be an effective way to showcase your communication style and personal interests.

Consistency Across Channels

Maintaining consistency across various digital channels is essential for creating a unified and recognizable brand image. This consistency helps in building trust and makes your personal brand easily identifiable to your audience. Here's how to achieve and maintain consistency across different platforms:

Defining Your Core Brand Elements:

- **Identify Key Brand Attributes:** Start by identifying the key elements of your brand, such as your core values, mission, and unique selling points. These should remain consistent across all channels.
- **Visual Identity:** Develop a consistent visual style, including colors, fonts, and imagery, that reflects your brand. Use this style across all your digital platforms, from your

website to your social media profiles.

Message Consistency:

- **Unified Messaging:** Ensure that your core message and tone of voice are consistent across different channels. Whether you're writing a blog post, tweeting, or updating your LinkedIn profile, your fundamental message should be aligned.
- **Adapting Without Losing Consistency:** While your message should be consistent, it's important to adapt your content to suit the format and audience of each platform. For example, the way you present your message on LinkedIn might be more formal compared to Twitter or Instagram.

Cross-Platform Branding:

- **Profile Harmonization:** Harmonize your profiles across different platforms. This includes using the same profile picture, bio, and background images where applicable.
- **Linking Between Channels:** Cross-promote your content and profiles by linking them together. For instance, include links to your social media on your blog or website and vice versa.

Content Strategy Alignment:

- **Coherent Content Themes:** Develop content themes that reflect your brand and use them consistently across channels. This doesn't mean posting the same content everywhere but rather exploring the same themes in different ways on different platforms.

- **Scheduling and Planning:** Use a content calendar to plan and schedule your posts across different channels. This helps in maintaining a consistent posting schedule and ensures your brand stays active and visible.

Monitoring and Adjusting Your Strategy:

- **Regular Audits:** Conduct regular audits of your digital presence. Check for consistency in messaging, visuals, and tone across all platforms.
- **Feedback and Adaptation:** Be open to feedback and willing to make adjustments. If certain elements of your brand are not resonating with your audience, be prepared to refine your approach while maintaining the core essence of your brand.

Monitoring Your Digital Footprint

Monitoring your digital footprint is a crucial aspect of personal branding, as it ensures that your online presence aligns with your professional goals and maintains a positive reputation. Here's how to effectively monitor and manage your digital footprint:

Regular Audits of Online Presence:

- **Google Yourself:** Start by searching for your name on popular search engines like Google. This will give you an idea of what information is readily available to anyone who searches for you.
- **Review Social Media Profiles:** Examine your social media profiles, ensuring that your bios, posts, and shared content remain consistent with your personal brand image.
- **Check for Inaccuracies:** Look for inaccuracies or outdated information. If you find any, take steps to correct or remove them.

Reputation Management:

- **Handling Negative Content:** If you come across negative content related to you or your brand, consider how to address it. Depending on the situation, this may involve responding professionally, requesting content removal, or seeking legal counsel if it's defamatory.
- **Leveraging Positive Content:** Highlight positive content about you. Share testimonials, endorsements, and positive reviews on your website and social media to build a favorable online reputation.

Privacy Settings and Online Security:

- **Adjust Privacy Settings:** Review and adjust privacy settings on your social media accounts and other online platforms. Limit the visibility of personal information to ensure your privacy.

- **Secure Your Accounts:** Implement strong passwords and enable two-factor authentication on all your accounts to protect them from unauthorized access.

Consistent Brand Image:

- **Alignment with Personal Brand:** Ensure that the content associated with your name aligns with your personal branding goals. It should reflect your values, expertise, and professional image.
- **Maintain Consistency:** Regularly update your profiles and content to reflect changes in your career or personal life. Consistency reinforces your brand identity.

Online Engagement and Interactions:

- **Engage Thoughtfully:** Be mindful of your interactions and comments on social media and other online platforms. Thoughtful engagement enhances your online reputation, while inflammatory or inappropriate comments can harm it.
- **Respond to Feedback:** Acknowledge feedback and criticism gracefully. Addressing constructive feedback professionally can demonstrate your commitment to self-improvement.

Monitoring Tools and Services:

- **Online Reputation Management Tools:** Consider using online reputation management tools and services that can help you track mentions of your name and brand across the internet. These tools can provide alerts about new content related to you.

- **Google Alerts:** Set up Google Alerts for your name and relevant keywords to receive notifications whenever new content is published online.

Regular Updates and Maintenance:

- **Ongoing Review:** Make monitoring your digital footprint an ongoing practice. Regularly review your online presence to ensure it remains aligned with your personal branding objectives.
- **Content Removal Requests:** If you find inaccurate or harmful content that you cannot control, consider contacting the platform or website owner to request removal.

5

Navigating Challenges and Pitfalls

W e will delve into strategies for navigating challenges and pitfalls that can arise in your personal branding journey.

Dealing with Negative Feedback and Trolls

Handling negative feedback and dealing with trolls is an inevitable part of maintaining an online presence. This section offers guidance on understanding feedback, addressing negative comments, and using criticism as an opportunity for growth:

Constructive vs. Destructive Feedback:

- **Identifying Constructive Feedback:** Learn to differentiate between constructive criticism and destructive comments. Constructive feedback is typically specific, actionable, and aimed at helping you improve.

- **Destructive Comments and Trolls:** Destructive comments are often characterized by insults, personal attacks, or baseless accusations. Trolls deliberately provoke and aim to disrupt online discussions.

Managing Negative Comments:

- **When to Respond:** Not all negative comments require a response. Evaluate whether the comment has merit and whether engaging will be productive. Respond if there's an opportunity for constructive dialogue.
- **Professionalism in Responses:** When responding, maintain professionalism and focus on addressing the issue raised rather than engaging in personal attacks. Keep your tone respectful and avoid emotional reactions.

Turning Negativity into Opportunity:

- **Seeking the Silver Lining:** Use negative feedback as an opportunity for improvement. Analyze the criticism objectively to identify areas where you can grow or refine your personal brand.
- **Public Response:** In some cases, responding publicly to criticism can demonstrate your commitment to transparency and improvement. Acknowledge the feedback and share the steps you plan to take.

Disengaging from Trolls:

- **Recognizing Trolls:** Trolls often seek attention and thrive on conflict. Recognize when you're dealing with a troll and consider whether it's best to disengage rather than fueling the fire.
- **Ignoring and Reporting:** Ignoring trolls can be an effective strategy. If their behavior persists or escalates, report them to the platform administrators for violation of community guidelines.

Fostering a Positive Online Community:

- **Moderating Comments:** If you manage a blog or social media page, consider moderating comments to filter out hateful or harmful content.
- **Setting Community Guidelines:** Establish clear community guidelines that outline acceptable behavior and interactions on your platform. Enforce these guidelines consistently.

Self-Care and Support:

- **Emotional Resilience:** Develop emotional resilience to handle negative feedback without it affecting your self-esteem. Seek support from friends, mentors, or support groups when needed.
- **Taking Breaks:** If negative comments become overwhelming, consider taking short breaks from social media to recharge and refocus on your goals.

Privacy and Security in the Digital Space

Maintaining privacy and security in the digital space is essential for protecting your personal brand and online identity. Here's a comprehensive guide on understanding and ensuring your privacy and security online:

Protecting Personal Information:

- **Strong Passwords:** Use strong, unique passwords for each online account. Password managers can help generate and store complex passwords.
- **Two-Factor Authentication (2FA):** Enable 2FA whenever possible to add an extra layer of security to your accounts.
- **Personal Data Minimization:** Be cautious about sharing personal information online. Only provide necessary information on public profiles and limit access to sensitive data.

Understanding Online Privacy:

- **Platform Privacy Settings:** Familiarize yourself with the privacy settings of each social media platform and adjust them according to your preferences. Control who can see your content and personal details.
- **Data Collection Awareness:** Understand how platforms collect and use your data. Review and adjust settings related to data sharing and tracking.

Avoiding Online Scams:

- **Phishing Awareness:** Be cautious of phishing attempts, which often involve fraudulent emails or websites attempting to steal your login credentials or personal information. Verify the legitimacy of any requests for sensitive information.
- **Online Purchases:** When making online purchases, ensure you're using reputable websites with secure payment methods. Be wary of fake online stores or scams.

Protecting Against Hacking:

- **Regular Software Updates:** Keep your operating system, applications, and antivirus software up to date to patch vulnerabilities.
- **Email Safety:** Avoid clicking on suspicious links or downloading attachments from unknown sources. Be cautious of email scams and phishing attempts.

Online Identity Management:

- **Use Pseudonyms:** Consider using pseudonyms or variations of your name for certain online accounts to limit the exposure of your full identity.
- **Online Persona vs. Personal Life:** Differentiate between your online persona and personal life. Share personal details sparingly, especially if they can be used to compromise your security.

Monitoring and Alerts:

- **Set Up Alerts:** Utilize services like Google Alerts or website monitoring tools to receive notifications about mentions of your name or personal brand online. This can help you stay aware of your digital footprint.
- **Monitoring Your Financials:** Regularly monitor your financial accounts for any suspicious activity.

Secure Communication:

- **Encrypted Messaging:** Use encrypted messaging apps for sensitive conversations to protect the privacy of your communications.
- **Secure File Sharing:** When sharing files or documents, use secure file-sharing methods and platforms with encryption.

Educate Yourself Continuously:

- **Stay Informed:** Stay informed about the latest online threats and security best practices. Regularly update your knowledge about online privacy and security.
- **Online Resources:** Utilize reputable online resources and organizations that provide guidance on digital privacy and security.

Overcoming Branding Mistakes

Everyone makes branding mistakes at some point in their personal branding journey. What sets successful personal brands apart is their ability to acknowledge and recover from these mistakes. Here's a guide on understanding and overcoming branding mistakes:

Recognizing Mistakes:

- **Self-Reflection:** Regularly evaluate your personal brand to identify any inconsistencies, missteps, or errors.
- **Feedback and Criticism:** Pay attention to feedback, both positive and negative. Constructive criticism can reveal areas where you may have made branding mistakes.

Taking Responsibility:

- **Ownership:** Accept responsibility for any branding mistakes. Avoid deflecting blame or making excuses.
- **Professionalism:** Handle any negative feedback or criticism with professionalism and grace.

Assessing the Impact:

- **Evaluate the Consequences:** Consider the impact of the mistake on your personal brand, reputation, and audience perception.
- **Severity:** Assess the severity of the mistake. Some mistakes may require immediate action, while others may be less damaging.

Learning from Errors:

- **Identify Lessons:** Determine what went wrong and why. Identify the specific aspects of your branding that need improvement.
- **Adaptation:** Use mistakes as opportunities for growth and adaptation. Adjust your branding strategy based on the lessons learned.

Apologizing and Making Amends:

- **Apologize Sincerely:** If the mistake has affected others or caused harm, offer a sincere apology. Acknowledge the impact of the mistake and express your commitment to making amends.
- **Correcting Mistakes:** Take appropriate steps to correct the mistake. This could involve deleting or revising content, clarifying your stance, or offering solutions.

Transparency and Authenticity:

- **Open Communication:** Be transparent with your audience about the mistake and your efforts to rectify it. Honest communication can help rebuild trust.
- **Authenticity:** Authenticity in admitting mistakes and working to rectify them is valued by audiences. Show your commitment to being genuine and transparent.

Rebuilding Trust:

- **Consistency:** Ensure that your actions align with your words and that you maintain consistency in your branding efforts moving forward.
- **Time and Patience:** Rebuilding trust takes time. Be patient and continue demonstrating your commitment to improvement.

Seeking Professional Help:

- **Rebranding:** In some cases, a complete rebrand may be necessary if the mistake has significantly damaged your personal brand. Seek professional assistance if needed.
- **Mentorship and Guidance:** Consider seeking guidance from mentors or professionals experienced in personal branding and reputation management.

Monitoring Progress:

- **Track Progress:** Continuously monitor your branding efforts and the impact of your corrections. Ensure that you are moving in a positive direction.
- **Feedback Loop:** Encourage feedback from your audience to gauge their perception and identify any lingering concerns.

Evolving Your Brand Over Time

Personal brands, like individuals, evolve and grow over time. It's essential to embrace change while maintaining your core values and authenticity. Here's a guide on understanding how to evolve your personal brand while staying true to your principles:

Recognizing the Need for Evolution:

- **Assess Your Goals:** Regularly assess your personal and professional goals. If your goals have evolved, it may be time to adjust your personal brand to align with them.
- **Audience and Industry Changes:** Pay attention to shifts in your audience's preferences and industry trends. Adapt to remain relevant.

Staying Authentic:

- **Core Values:** Identify your core values and principles that define your personal brand. These should remain consistent even as you evolve.
- **Authenticity:** Maintain authenticity in your branding efforts. Be true to yourself and your values, and let them guide your evolution.

Gradual vs. Radical Changes:

- **Gradual Evolution:** Consider gradual changes that align with your long-term vision. This approach allows you to evolve while minimizing the risk of alienating your existing audience.

- **Radical Rebranding:** In some cases, a radical rebrand may be necessary to reflect significant changes in your goals or identity. Seek professional guidance for a successful rebrand.

Communication and Transparency:

- **Open Dialogue:** Communicate with your audience about your evolution. Share your reasons for change and how it benefits them.
- **Transparent Changes:** Be transparent about the changes you're making in your personal brand. This fosters trust and understanding.

Maintaining Consistency:

- **Consistent Messaging:** While evolving, ensure that your messaging remains consistent with your updated personal brand. Your core values should still shine through.
- **Visual Identity:** If you have visual branding elements (such as logos or color schemes), consider whether they need updates to align with your evolving brand.

Professional Growth and Learning:

- **Invest in Learning:** Invest in continuous learning and personal development. Demonstrating growth in your skills and knowledge enhances your personal brand.
- **Share Insights:** Share your learning journey and insights with your audience. This can position you as a thought

leader in your field.

Feedback and Adaptation:

- **Feedback Loop:** Encourage feedback from your audience regarding your evolving brand. Their input can provide valuable insights and help you make adjustments.
- **Adapt to Feedback:** Be open to feedback and willing to adapt based on audience preferences and expectations.

Measuring Success:

- **Define Success Metrics:** Clearly define the metrics that indicate the success of your evolving personal brand. These could include audience growth, engagement rates, or achieving specific career milestones.
- **Regular Assessment:** Continuously assess your progress toward these metrics to ensure that your evolution is on track.

6

Case Studies and Success Stories

How to engage with real-world examples and insights to provide valuable lessons in personal branding.

Interviews with Successful Personal Brands

In this section, we teach you how to create interviews with individuals who have successfully established and maintained compelling personal brands. These interviews should provide valuable insights into the diverse perspectives and strategies that have contributed to their success.

Diverse Perspectives:

- **Varied Industries:** The individuals featured in these interviews come from a range of industries, including business, arts, technology, and more. Explore these interviews to gain a comprehensive understanding of personal branding in different fields.

- **Career Paths:** Each interviewee has followed a unique career path, from entrepreneurs to artists to thought leaders. Their experiences offer valuable lessons regardless of your own career stage.

Behind-the-Scenes Insights:

- **Real Stories:** These interviews go beyond surface-level success stories. They delve into the challenges, setbacks, and personal growth journeys of these individuals.
- **Strategies and Tactics:** Learn about the specific strategies and tactics they used to build and maintain their personal brands. Identify actionable takeaways that align with your goals.

Key Questions to Consider:

- **What Motivated Them:** Explore the motivations and driving forces behind each individual's personal brand. Understanding their motivations can help you align your own branding efforts with your goals.
- **Challenges Overcome:** Pay attention to the challenges they faced and how they overcame them. This can provide insights into resilience and problem-solving in personal branding.
- **Lessons from Setbacks:** Discover the lessons they learned from setbacks or failures. These lessons can help you navigate challenges more effectively.

Application to Your Brand:

- **Analyze Parallels:** Consider how the experiences and strategies of these successful individuals parallel or contrast with your own personal brand journey. Identify areas where you can apply their insights.
- **Adaptation:** Personalize the lessons from these interviews to suit your unique circumstances and goals. Adapt their strategies to your specific industry and audience.

Inspiration and Motivation:

- **Drawing Inspiration:** Use these interviews as a source of inspiration and motivation. Hearing about the achievements of others can fuel your own aspirations.
- **Building Confidence:** Recognize that success is achievable with dedication and strategic personal branding efforts. These interviews can boost your confidence in your branding journey.

Analysis of Effective Digital Branding Strategies

In this section, we dissect and analyze the strategies employed by successful personal brands featured in the book. It offers valuable insights into the key components that have contributed to their success in the digital realm. Here's how to understand and apply the different strategies and case studies:

Comprehensive Strategy Breakdown:

- **Identify Core Strategies:** Each case study provides an in-depth look at the core strategies used by successful personal brands. Pay close attention to these strategies, as they form the foundation of effective digital branding.
- **Segmented Analysis:** Break down the strategies into segments, such as content creation, audience engagement, platform selection, and online presence management. This segmentation allows for a detailed understanding of each aspect.

Practical Takeaways:

- **Actionable Insights:** Extract actionable takeaways from each case study. Look for specific tactics, approaches, and methods that can be applied to your own personal branding efforts.
- **Implementable Advice:** Identify strategies that align with your goals and resources. Choose those that are realistically implementable in your context.

Case Studies in Context:

- **Industry Relevance:** Consider the industry or niche of the personal brands being analyzed. Recognize how certain strategies are tailored to specific industries and audiences.
- **Adaptability:** While industry-specific strategies are valuable, look for universal principles that can be adapted across various fields.

Measuring Success:

- **Success Metrics:** Understand the metrics and indicators of success used in each case study. Determine how success was measured and track these metrics in your own branding efforts.
- **Benchmarking:** Use the case studies as benchmarks to assess your progress. Compare your results against the success stories to identify areas for improvement.

Holistic Approach:

- **360-Degree Perspective:** Consider the holistic approach to personal branding. Understand how various strategies work together to create a cohesive and impactful brand.
- **Integration:** Explore how strategies like content creation, audience engagement, and online presence management are integrated to reinforce the personal brand's message and identity.

Adaptation and Innovation:

- **Adaptation:** Recognize that strategies evolve over time, and what worked for a particular personal brand may require adaptation to fit changing digital landscapes.
- **Innovation:** Encourage innovative thinking and experimentation within your own branding efforts. Case studies often highlight instances of creative and unique approaches.

Personalization:

- **Tailor Strategies:** While learning from case studies, consider how you can tailor strategies to your unique personality, strengths, and brand identity. Personalization is key to authenticity.
- **Balancing Act:** Balance between adopting successful strategies and infusing your brand with your personal touch. Strive for a balance that aligns with your values.

Lessons Learned from Branding Failures

This section focuses on the valuable lessons that can be gleaned from branding failures and setbacks. Understanding these lessons is crucial for avoiding common pitfalls and turning challenges into opportunities for growth. Here's how to comprehend and apply the lessons learned from branding failures:

Identifying Common Pitfalls:

- **Recognize the Mistakes:** Analyze the branding failures highlighted in the case studies. Identify the common mistakes or missteps made by individuals in their personal branding journeys.
- **Avoiding Repetition:** Understand how these mistakes can be detrimental to your own personal brand and make a conscious effort to avoid them.

Adaptation and Resilience:

- **Embracing Change:** Acknowledge that setbacks and failures are part of any personal branding journey. Embrace change and be open to adapting your brand strategy when necessary.
- **Resilience:** Learn from the individuals who faced failures and yet managed to bounce back stronger. Cultivate resilience as an essential quality in personal branding.

Preventing and Mitigating Failures:

- **Risk Awareness:** Develop a keen awareness of potential risks and challenges in personal branding. Anticipate issues that may arise and proactively address them.
- **Recovery Strategies:** Understand the strategies employed by individuals to recover from branding failures. Learn how they turned negative experiences into opportunities for growth.

Transparency and Honesty:

- **Transparent Communication:** Emulate the transparency displayed by those who openly acknowledged their failures. If you encounter setbacks, communicate honestly with your audience about the situation.
- **Authenticity:** Maintain authenticity even when addressing failures. Authenticity in acknowledging mistakes can help rebuild trust.

Continuous Learning:

- **Growth Mindset:** Develop a growth mindset that values learning from failures. See failures as opportunities for improvement and learning.
- **Iterative Improvement:** Use the lessons learned to iterate and improve your personal branding strategy over time. Make adjustments based on your experiences and feedback.

Audience Perception:

- **Audience Reaction:** Consider how the audience reacted to the failures and subsequent recovery efforts. Understand the impact of failures on audience perception.
- **Rebuilding Trust:** Take deliberate steps to rebuild trust and credibility with your audience after a branding failure.

Preemptive Measures:

- **Preventative Strategies:** Explore strategies that can pre-emptively mitigate the risk of branding failures. Proactive measures can help you avoid potential pitfalls.
- **Consultation and Mentorship:** Seek guidance from mentors or experts who can provide insights on avoiding common branding mistakes.

Balancing Innovation and Caution:

- **Innovation:** While learning from failures, continue to innovate and experiment with your personal brand. Don't let the fear of failure stifle creativity.

- **Caution:** Balance innovation with caution by learning from the mistakes of others. Be strategic in your branding efforts to minimize risks.

7

Conclusion

I t's essential to reflect on the transformative journey we've embarked on together. This book has been your pocket guide to navigating the digital landscape with confidence, building a personal brand that resonates with your values, goals, and audience. Throughout this journey, we've explored the depths of personal branding, from understanding your digital identity to effectively leveraging different platforms, and from analyzing successful case studies to learning from branding failures.

Our vision for this book was to empower professionals, entrepreneurs, freelancers, and digital enthusiasts with the knowledge, strategies, and insights necessary to excel in the online world. We've delved into the intricacies of personal branding, ensuring that you not only grasp the concepts but also know how to apply them in practical terms.

In your pursuit of mastering your digital identity, you've discovered the importance of authenticity, the significance of consistent messaging, and the power of audience engagement. You've learned to navigate challenges, embrace change, and even turn setbacks into stepping stones toward growth. Your digital footprint is no longer a mystery but a canvas where you paint your unique brand proposition.

Now, as you move forward on your personal branding journey, remember that growth is a continuous process. Embrace every opportunity to learn, adapt, and innovate. Share your insights and experiences with others, fostering a community of like-minded individuals dedicated to personal and professional development.

But before you turn the final page, here's a small request. If "Digital Identity Unlocked" has enriched your understanding of personal branding and provided you with actionable strategies, we invite you to leave a review on Amazon. Your review can help fellow readers discover the value of this book and embark on their own journey of mastering their digital identity.

Thank you for joining us on this empowering journey of personal branding. Your digital identity is now unlocked, and the online world awaits your authentic and impactful presence. Go forth with confidence, purpose, and a clear understanding of your personal brand, and make your mark in the digital landscape.

Now, let's put everything into action. Your journey has just begun, and the possibilities are limitless.

If you are interested in learning more about digital marketing, check out The Roadmap, the ultimate digital marketing course to generate low-maintenance income through social media at:

https://stan.store/TheDigitalPalette/p/roadmap-hh08